Looking at Flowers

Written by Frances Lee

A Haights Cross Communications Company

Look at these flowers.

Look at this flower.
It is yellow.

It looks like the sun.

Here is a purple flower.
What does it look like?

It looks like a bell.

Look at the red flower.
What does it look like?

It looks like a brush.

What does this white flower look like?

It looks like a star.

Here is a pink flower.
What does it look like?

It looks like a cup.

What does this orange
flower look like?

It looks like a bird.

What do these flowers
look like?

alphakids

guiding young readers in literacy

AlphaKids Plus
Books for Emergent Reading

Word count **Looking at Flowers**: 89

**alphakids®
plus**

Books at Level 5

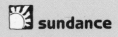
sundance

ISBN 0-7608-6551-5

9 780760 865514

21740